Table of Contents

Mathematics: An Effective Means of Solving Problems

We invite you to take a journey way back in time, in the year 1895. We are inside one of the best universities attending a Physics lecture conducted by the Faculty of Engineering.

The professor takes a metallic sphere and, with the aid of a machine, throws it into the air. He tells the students the initial speed of the sphere as it exits the machine, its angle of trajectory in relation to the ground, and the mass of the sphere. He asks them to calculate the distance over which the sphere could travel.

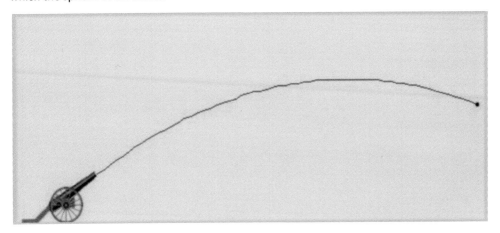

The students are very much aware that to find the solution to this problem, they must use the second-order quadratic equation for the trajectory:

$$y(x) = \frac{-g}{2v_0^2 \cos^2 \theta} x^2 + \tan \theta x$$

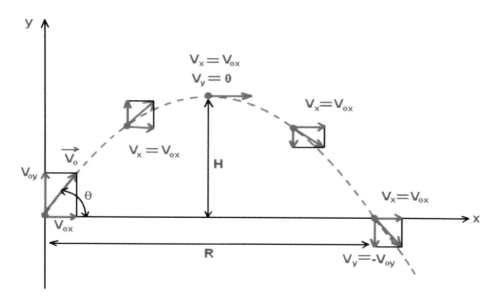

To determine how long the object remains in the air before it falls, the students must apply this formula:

t = 2V0sinθ/g

To know the distance the object can travel in the air, the students must apply this formula:

R = v20sin/2θg

A student asks the professor if he thinks that an object that is heavier than air could be used as a means of air transportation in the years to come. The lecturer, as well as the other students, thinks that he is daringly ignorant to harbor such a stupid thought. The professor tells him that it is impossible for a body that is heavier than air to fly and land. As a result, it cannot be used as a means of air transportation.

If anyone builds a device that is heavier than the air and thinks that he can make it fly in the same way that this metallic sphere remained in the air for only a short period of time, a flying machine would remain in the air for the same short duration and its trajectory and the exact crash site could be calculated.

The professor goes on to say, "Some people who have no scientific training believe and continue to think that this is possible. However, we who have a high level of academic achievement know that an object that is heavier than air cannot be used for air transport.

Certainly, a body like a balloon, which contains a light gas such as hydrogen or helium, can be made to fly; but to make an object that is heavier than air into a means of air transportation is scientifically impossible," the professor concludes.

Figure 1: Gonaïves after the application of the formula

Bernoulli's Formula

Wright brother airplane model

We are now in 1903, specifically December 17, 1903. Two brothers, Orville and Wilbur Wright, have just built a flying machine. They sit inside it, they make it fly and land, contrary to what the educated people of that time believed. Given this scientific problem, thinkers began to understand the nature of this dilemma in order to find an explanation. The strategy they used was to put the problem on paper, to translate it into mathematical language, to come up with a solution, to take this solution and apply it to a flying machine. By putting the problem on paper, we are able to solve it by applying Bernoulli's theorem to it.

$$p1 + 1/2\varrho V12 + \varrho gz1 = p2 + 1/2\varrho V22 + \varrho gz2 = p + 1/2\varrho V2 + \varrho gz = \text{Constant}$$

Several people in Haiti understand the concept of this theorem well without having studied it and without even knowing its name. Some children in Haiti who grew up in the coastal towns or in towns through which rivers pass know how to make little paper boats. They put these boats in the river and make them float along with the tide.

Let us put two little boats, boat A and boat B side by side but separated by a certain distance. We are going to visualize these boats in the River Limbé which is shown below. We make them take off at the same time. Boat A moves towards one of the rocks in the river. Boat B goes in the same direction as boat A but parallel and at some distance of the stone. We observe that boat A must cover a greater distance than boat B because it must go around the rock while boat B goes straight ahead. However, after leaving the rock behind, the two boats arrive at the same time. Taking into account the fact that boat A had to cover a longer distance, it must also move a lot faster to meet up with boat B after going past the rock.

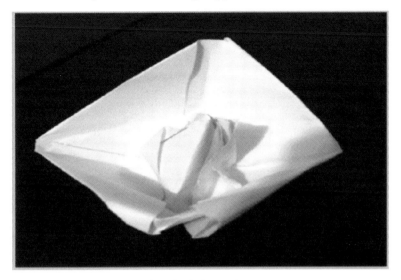

Figure 2: A little paper boat

Figure 3: River Limbé in Haiti

The formula above illustrates the two boats on the river. Aircrafts fly based on this same principle. The boat is to the water what the airplane is to the air. The rocks in the river represent the wings of the airplane. In the river, a wave can displace or move little boats from one point to another; an airplane has one or several engines that push its wings through the air. Boats "A" and "B" represent the molecules of air which go above and below the wings.

The molecules of air which pass above the wing of the aircraft must cover a distance that is longer than that which the molecules passing beneath the wings cover. The molecules of air which pass above and beneath the wing obey Bernoulli's law. The molecules of air which pass above the wings have a high speed while having a lower pressure compared to the molecules which pass beneath the wing.

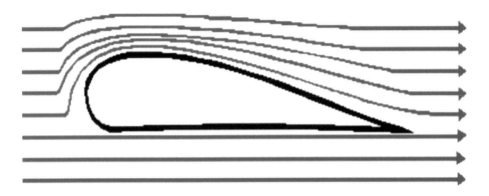

The fact that the pressure above the airplane's wing is lower than the pressure beneath it triggers the creation of an upward pull. This is exactly what happens when we suck on coconut water with a straw: the coconut water comes up into the mouth by suction. In the case of an aircraft, the wings of an aircraft are pulled up by the difference in pressure between the upper and the lower surfaces of the wing.

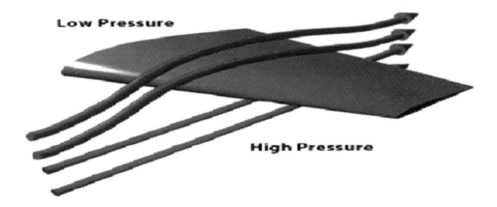

Let's go through the essential points of our journey in time: Initially, it was believed that air transportation was mathematically impossible. Somebody flew an airplane contrary to what the scientific world then believed. The scientific world had put the problem on paper and translated it into mathematical language. On the basis of this mathematical language, they were able to find a solution and to manipulate the results. Finally, they can design an airplane today that is capable of conveying a lot of people from one point to another.

A Formula for Solving Haiti's Problem

Haitians have not stopped declining since their great victory over Bonaparte's army. Haiti, once called the Pearl of the Antilles and the first independent republic of coloured people, is today the poorest country on the American continent. Following the example of scientists in 1903, it is time for us to put Haiti's problem on paper and derive the mathematical formula to arrive at a solution which will allow the country to take its place among industrialized countries. The formula must be very simple and it must be understood by the majority of Haitians, no matter their intellectual capacity.

The formula that we will use is called "the formula for the development of Haiti":

$A = X1(C) + X2(E) - X3(L1) - X4(L2)$

where

X1 is the Selling Price of local products

X2 is the Selling Price of exported products

X3 is the Cost price of international items

X4 is the Cost price of imported finished goods

C is the Local consumption

E is the Exported finished products

L1 is the imported items

L2 is the imported finished products

We can also write this formula in a more explicit manner.

A = (Sale of local products) + (Sale of exported products) - (Purchases of imported items) – (Purchases of imported finished products)

When the value of A is positive, we could say "Haiti is a developed country".

A <==> Haiti is developed

Figure 4: Apartment building in Les Cayes

This formula may also be seen as a triangle whose three sides are:

1. Haiti must produce a lot
2. Haiti must export a lot
3. Haiti must import a little

Figure 5: Port-au-Prince after the application of the formula

Exercises to Facilitate the Understanding of the Formula

Although the formula is very simple, it is helpful to do at least two exercises to make us fully understand how to manipulate the "formula for the development of Haiti."

In the first exercise, we invite you to 1) consider a problem in plain language, 2) translate it into mathematical language and then 3) solve it in order to translate the mathematical solution back into our everyday vocabulary.

Exercise 1: John has a mango tree. The mango tree can yield a random number of ripe mangoes per day: 2, 4, 0, 5, 1, etc. Yesterday, there were no ripe mangoes. He, therefore, borrowed 2 ripe mangoes from his neighbour Peter. Today, his mango tree yielded 5 ripe mangoes. Peter comes to claim back the 2 ripe mangoes he had given to John yesterday. How many ripe mangoes would John have to eat today?

$A = B + C$

A= Number of ripe mangoes that John will eat today

B= Number of ripe mangoes that the tree yields today

C= Number of ripe mangoes that Peter lent John yesterday.

By applying our mathematical formula to arrive at the solution, we get:

$A = B + C$

Number of mangoes that John will eat today = (the 5 ripe mangoes that John's mango tree yielded today) less (the 2 ripe mangoes that John must return to Peter) equals 3 mangoes

$A = (5 \text{ mangoes}) + (-2 \text{ mangoes})$
$A = (5 \text{ mangoes}) + (-2 \text{ mangoes})$
$A = (5 \text{ mangoes}) - (2 \text{ mangoes}) = 3 \text{ mangoes}$
$A = (5) + (-2) = 3$
$A = 5-2 = 3$
$A = 3$
Therefore, the solution is:
A= John will now eat 3 mangoes.

Exercise 2: In the first exercise, we have seen that $A = 5 - 2$ which had been interpreted as follows: John had 5 ripe mangoes and he took out 2 of these 5 ripe mangoes, the 2 which he owed to Peter. John is, therefore, left with 3 ripe mangoes to eat. The question now is: Is it possible to take out 5 ripe mangoes from 2 ripe mangoes (5-2)?

Let us consider the problem together!

Yesterday, John's mango tree yielded no ripe mango. John, therefore, asked his neighbour Peter to lend him 5 ripe mangoes to eat. Today, John's mango tree yielded 2 ripe mangoes. Peter came to ask for the 5 ripe mangoes which he lent to John yesterday. How many ripe mangoes would John be able to eat today?

Figure 6: The city of Ounaminthe after the application of the formula

When we express that in mathematical terms, we get:

A= B + C

A = Number of mangoes that John ate today

B = Number of ripe mangoes that the mango tree yielded today

C = Number of ripe mangoes that Peter had given John yesterday

Can John give back the 5 ripe mangoes to Peter? How would Peter react? Would Peter tell John not to bother about the 5 ripe mangoes, considering that he couldn't possibly give them back? If we admit that we cannot take out 5 ripe mangoes from 2 ripe mangoes, we also imply that Peter does not have the right to demand 5 ripe mangoes from John. Must Peter lose his 5 ripe mangoes? Must we put John in prison because he could not return the 5 ripe mangoes?

Can we arrive at a mathematical solution to this problem? Of course. The mathematical language is a good way to solve even the most complex problems.

By applying the formula of the previous problem, we have:

A = B + C

A = (the 2 ripe mangoes that the mango tree yielded to John today) and (the 5 ripe mangoes that John took from Peter)

A = (2 mangoes) + (- 5 mangoes)

A = (2 mangoes) – (5 mangoes) = -3

A = 2 + (-5)

A = 2-5

A = -3, A is negative

A = John has no more mangoes to eat today and on top of that, he has a debt of 3 mangoes.

Figure 7: Martissant Shopping Centre after the application of the formula

In common parlance, we interpret the preceding mathematical solution as follows:

Peter came to John and tells him "Give me the 5 ripe mangoes that you owe me." John replies, "I don't have 5 ripe mangoes; I have only 2 ripe mangoes. I am going to give you 2 ripe mangoes now and I will owe you 3 ripe mangoes." As a result, A = -3, the minus sign indicates that John gives Peter 2 ripe mangoes, and that he still owes Peter 3 ripe mangoes in order to pay his debt. Aside from that, John would have no more ripe mangoes to eat today.

In the formula A = B + C, we can, therefore, see that A can be positive and A can also be negative.

In the next chapter, we will see why sometimes, we have a positive A and at other times, we have a negative A.

Figure 8: Hinche after the application of the formula

How to Manipulate the Formula

In the preceding chapter, we have seen how "A" may be positive and how it may also be negative. In this chapter, we are going to see how we can manipulate the formula to arrive at the desired result. In other words, how we can convert negative results into positive results. To understand the formula better, let us continue with more examples.

This time, instead of mangoes, we will use our national currency - the "gourd".

A = amount of gourds in the house.

When A is positive, (A) refers to the money we have, which we possess. When A is negative, (-A) represents the money we owe, which is our debt.

The three situations below make A have a negative value.

Scenario 1: If B is negative and C is negative, A will be negative.

B: John has bought pistachio nuts from a trader on credit for 10 gourds.

C: Peter, his neighbour, has made him a trouser for 60 gourds.

Since B and C are both debts, B and C are negative; therefore, A is also going to be negative.

Let us apply the formula A = B + C.

A = (The 10 gourds which John must pay for the pistachio nuts) plus (the 60 gourds which he must pay Peter for the trousers)
A = (-10 gourds) + (-60 gourds)
A = -70 gourds
Therefore, A is negative.

Scenario 2: If B is lower than C, and B is positive while C is negative, the result will be negative.

B: John has 40 gourds.

C: Peter asks his neighbour to pay him an old debt of 100 gourds.

To find A, we apply the same formula A = B + C

A = (John has 40 gourds) and (his neighbour Peter asks him to pay up a debt of 100 gourds)
A = (40 gourds) + (-100 gourds)
A = 60 gourds
John has a deficit of 60 gourds; therefore, A is negative.

Scenario 3: If B is higher than C, and B is negative while C is positive, the result will be negative.

B: A friend lends John 200 gourds.

C: Peter, the neighbour, just paid John 110 gourds for a job that he had done.

To apply our formula A = B + C

A = (200 gourds which the friend lent to John) plus (the 110 gourds paid to John for the work which he did)
A = (-200 gourds) + (110 gourds)
A = -90 gourds
Therefore, A is negative.

Figure 9: City of Cap-Haitien after the application of the formula

The following three situations make A have a positive value.

Scenario 1: If B is positive and C is positive, A will be positive.

B: John has 50 gourds.
C: Peter, his neighbour, must pay him 30 gourds for the painting work he had done.
A = (50 gourds which John has) plus (the 30 gourds for the painting work he did for his
    neighbour Peter)
A = (50 gourds) + (30 gourds)
A = 80 gourds
Therefore, A is positive.

Scenario 2: If B is higher than C, and B is positive while C is negative, A will be positive.
B: John has 600 gourds.
C: John's neighbour, Peter, asks for the 40 gourds he lent to John.
By applying our formula A = B + C:
A = (600 gourds which John has) plus (40 gourds lent to John)
A = (600 gourds) + (-40 gourds)
A = 600 gourds - 40 gourds = 560 gourds
A = 560 gourds
Therefore, A is positive.

Scenario 3: If B is lower than C, and B is negative while C is positive, A will be positive.
B: John owes his brother Luc 100 gourds.
C: Peter just gave John 700 gourds for the rent of a room.
By applying the formula A = B + C, we have:
A = (The debt of 100 gourds from John and his brother Luc) plus (the 700 gourds which John
received from Peter for the rent of the room)
A = (-100 gourds) + (700 gourds)
A = -100 gourds + 700 gourds
A = 600 gourds
We can also write it as follows:
A = 700 gourds - 100 gourds
A = 600 gourds
Therefore, A is positive.

Figure 10: Saint-Marc after the application of the formula

Understanding "The Formula for the Development of Haiti"

With the preceding exercises, we can now understand and apply the "formula for development" to the Haiti situation. In fact, Haiti now has a negative A, which means that it is a poor country. We will not use the formula as a thermometer but rather as a thermostat. A thermometer indicates the value of the temperature while a thermostat changes the level of the temperature. This is to say that we will not apply the formula to Haiti just to obtain Haiti's current economic level, which will naturally indicate that Haiti is a poor country (in essence, we don't need any formula to know that Haiti IS a poor country). We simply need to apply it to modify the result, to convert the negative A into a positive A, to make Haiti go from being a poor country into being a rich one.

Figure 11: The Grand'Anse River at Jeremie after the application of the formula

No country is destined to be perpetually rich. During the colonial era, Spain had about 70% of all the gold in the world. Currently, Spain is far from being a rich country. The reverse is also true: no country is condemned to perpetual poverty. Haiti is currently the poorest country in the Americas. It can become one of the richest countries but for this to become a reality, Haitians must agree to apply the "formula for development" in order to it from a poor country into a rich one.

To understand the meaning of this formula, one of the examples showed us that the positive or negative value of A determined whether or not John could eat mangoes. It should also be observed that whenever A is negative, it means that "John will go to bed without eating mangoes", but not necessarily that he would go to bed on an empty stomach. In reality, even if John has no mangoes to eat, as long as there are other kinds of food at home, he would not be hungry on that day.

In the same way, by using the "formula for the development of Haiti", if Haiti has a negative A in one product, it does not mean that Haiti is a poor country because of that. The positive or negative A indicates that a country is poor or rich on the basis of the total sum of all its products, and not just a single product. In other words, Haiti will be a rich country when the sum of its products yields a positive A. In the same manner, Haiti presently has a negative A because the sum of all its products yields a negative A.

Figure 12: Côtes-de-Fer after the application of the formula

Application of the "Formula for the Development of Haiti"

We are going to apply the formula to a single product—rice—but in 4 different situations. In the first case, we will consider the fact that we produce less rice than the people need.

The formula for the development of Haiti is

$A = X1(C) + X2(E) - X3(L1) - X4(L2)$

where

X1 is the Selling Price of local products

X2 is the Selling Price of exported products

X3 is the Cost Price of international items

X4 is the Cost Price of imported finished goods

C is the Local Consumption

E is the Exported finished products

L1 is the imported items

L2 is the imported finished products

A = (Sale of local products) + (Sale of exported products) – (Purchases of imported products) – (Purchases of imported finished products)

Problem: Haitian farmers will plant rice at Artibonite and at Acul-du-Sud and they must feed a region which needs 5000 bags of rice. The farmers, instead of 5000 bags, produced only 800 bags. The traders will sell 1 kg of rice for $0.03. The ministry in charge of Agriculture knows that it must offer a good quality product. In other words, we wouldn't want to give the consumer rice that is mixed with small stones. Furthermore, they must import a lot of branded bags from abroad for the storage of rice produced in Haiti. The price of each branded bag is $0.45.

We recall that 5000 bags need to be provided to the region. The local production is not enough because the farmers have produced only 800 bags of rice. Thus, a decision needs to be made:

a) We could say that we are not bothered about the missing 4200 bags of rice need to completely feed the assigned zone. If someone doesn't eat, that is his/her problem.
b) We can also choose to import rice to feed the entire zone.

We have chosen the second solution.

Local selling price X1 = $ 0.30 per kg

Cost price of imported items (Empty bags) X3 = $ 0.45

Price of imported products X4 = $ 1.44

Quantity of rice produced P = 800 bags of rice

Imported items (empty bags) C1 = 5000 bags

Imported finished products L1 = 800 branded bags.

Applying the formula

A = (sale of indigenous products) + (sale of exported products) – (purchases of imported items) - (purchases of imported finished products)

The farmers have produced only 800 bags of rice.

Figure 13: The Borneau Lammare National School after the application of the formula

(Sale of local products): $0.30 x 800 = $240.00

We must first produce food to provide 5000 bags of rice.

(Sale of exported products) = 0

We must put the rice in bags. According to the example, we do not produce bags in Haiti, and must therefore import them. We import 800 bags in order to fill them with our local rice.

(Purchases of imported products): $0.45 x 800 = $360.00 We need 5,000 bags of rice, but the country produces only 800 bags. Consequently, we must import

4200 (5000 – 800 = 4200) bags of rice. The price of imported rice is $1.44.

(Purchases of imported products): $1.44 x 4200 = $6048.00

We will find the value of A by applying the formula

A = (Sale of local products) + (Sale of exported products) – (purchases of imported items) - (purchases of imported finished products)

A = ($240) + (0) – ($360) – ($6,048)
A = -$6168
A is negative.

Here is the second solution:

The leaders understood that one way of changing the negative A into a positive is to encourage farmers to produce more rice. This time, the farmers succeeded in harvesting a total of 5550 bags of rice. Therefore, we have something to export abroad.

We recall that farmers need to provide the zone with 5000 bags of rice. However, they have produced much more than that, i.e., 5550 bags of rice. Initially, they will dispose the 5000 bags of rice to satisfy the local demand and it will be sold at $0.30 per kilogram.

(Sale of local products): $0.30 x 5000 = $1500.00

In the preceding case, we had not produced enough rice to satisfy the local demand; we did not have the possibility of exporting. This time, after satisfying the local consumption, we still have 500 (5500-5000) bags of rice available. We will, therefore, export. The selling price for exports abroad is $1.30.

(Sale of exported products): $1.30 x 500 = $650.00

We must put the rice produced in Haiti into 5500 bags which we have purchased. We recall that the price of each bag was $0.45.

(Purchases of imported items (bags)): $0.45 x 5500 = $2475.00

The local production is so great that we don't have any need to import rice from abroad.

The city of Jacmel

Figure 14: City of Jacmel after the application of the formula

(Purchases of imported products) = 0

Let us find A by applying the formula:
A= ($1500) + ($650)-($2475)-($0) A = -$325.00
A is still negative.

The farmers have made great effort to produce so much rice to the point of having a substantial quantity to export abroad. However, A is still negative. We realize that to have a positive A, the less we produce, the less we must import. A strategy that aims at maintaining a positive A is to reduce imports as much as possible.

We can reduce our imports in the following situations. One good way to do it is, rather than buying bags from abroad, we would only buy fabric from abroad and then make the bags in Haiti. With this change, instead of spending $2,475.00 ($0.45 x 5500) on bags, we spend only $550 (5500 x $0.10).

By applying the formula, we have the following result:

$A = X_1(C) + X_2(E) - X_3(L_1) - X_4(L_2)$

A= (Sale of local products) + (sale of exported products)-(Purchases of imported items)-(Purchases of finished imported products)

(Sale of local products): $0.30 x 5000 = $1500.0
(Sale of exported products): $1.30 =$650.00
(Purchases of imported materials (bags)): $0.10 x 5500 = $550.00

This time, we don't need all the rice!

(Purchases of imported products): 0

A= ($1500.00) + ($650.00)-($550.00)-(0)
A= $1600
We have a positive A simply by reducing imports.

Previously, we harvested much more rice than we did. In the first situation, A was still negative. In the second situation, we have reduced imports and the negative A has become positive.

Figure 15: Hotel at Anse-a-Galets after the application of the formula

Scenario 2: This time, we will increase the value of A via the production of more rice. Instead of 5500 bags of rice, we will produce 9000 bags of rice.

We must provide 5000 bags of rice to our local market. The price of rice at the point of purchase would be $0.30 per kilogram.

(Sale of local products): $0.30 x 5000 = $1500.0

We have greater production this time around. We now have 4000 (9000-5000) bags of rice to export abroad:

(Sale of exported products) = $1.30 x 4000 = $5200.00

We must invest in 9000 empty bags to put the rice for local consumption as well as the rice that for export. Given that we have not imported the rice bags from abroad, but only the fabric for making the bags in Haiti, the cost of the bags is reduced to $0.10 per bag:

(Purchases of imported items): $0.10 x 9000 = $900.00

This time, we don't have to import rice because the local production is more than enough.
(Purchases of imported products): 0

Let us apply the formula:
A = (Sale of local products) + (sale of exported products)- (purchases of imported items)- (Purchases of imported finished products)
A = ($1500) + ($5200)-($900)-($0)

A = $5800.00
A is still positive with a greater value.

We have seen from this scenario that the farmers harvested much more rice than the local demand. Thus, by reducing importation to its lowest level, we have made A positive.

Figure 16: City of Petit-Goave after the application of the formula

Our Products on the International Market

It is good to note that it is one thing to have enough products for exportation to another country and it is another thing to find a country which would need our products. Besides, whenever we find a country which would need rice, other countries with surplus rice would equally try to sell it to that country.

Let us take Cuba, for example. It needs to import rice. We can offer our surplus rice, but Mexico also has surplus rice. Cuba will take at least two factors into consideration to make a decision:

- The quality of rice that they wish to buy
- The amount of money to be invested into importing it.

Figure 17: Baradères after the application of the formula

Figure 18: City of Port-de-Paix after the application of the formula

We can be competitive with Mexico at the level of quality, but it is almost impossible at the level of price. A great advantage which they have over us is in the area of production. The land area over which production takes place is a lot bigger, which causes us to offer a more expensive product.

We will take the example of a rice-producing country which produces enough food to feed the whole nation and enough to export abroad. If all countries with which this rice-producing country has trade relations produce enough rice to feed their people, nobody would need to buy from this rice-producing country. This would then be a loss for this rice-producing country. Consequently, it will therefore be in its interest that the country which buys from it does not produce enough rice.

If Haiti does not produce enough rice to sell to the whole population in Haiti, it is of great economic interest to the rice producer which needs to sell its rice.

If this rice-producing country could discourage rice production in Haiti, what would this mean for the rice-producing country? According to the Global index (http://www.indexmundi.com), the Haitian population was 9,996,731. We will consider that out of this 9,996,731 people, only 600,000 Haitians buy 20lbs of "fortified long grain rice", (20lbs, 9071 lb = 8474 kilogram) at $9.00 monthly. The rice-producing country earns US$5,400,000.00 per month ($9 x 600,000 = $5,400,000.00). In the course of the year, the country would earn US $64,800,000.00 (US 5,400,000.00 x 12 = 64,800,000). Is it in the interest of the rice-producing country if Haiti produces enough rice to feed its inhabitants? Certainly not! Its interest is to discourage our local production. It can even claim to establish agricultural programs precisely to divert Haiti from its goal, which is the production of enough rice to feed all Haitians.

The Need to Reduce Importation

We have used the rice example in the application of our formula. However, the production of rice only, however, would never get us out of our current economic crisis. Besides, our limited territory does not allow us to develop agriculture to its fullest.

To sell our product on the global market, we must become competitive. It is compulsory to offer a good-quality product at a competitive price. If two countries use the same plantation technique, the one which has more land would be in the position to produce more, and the result would be a less costly product.

It would be almost impossible to compete against a country which has a land area that is bigger than ours. However, we have the agricultural capacity to feed all of our compatriots who live in Haiti without the need for imports.

A means of feeding the Haitian people would be to choose commercial production instead of everybody randomly planting something in his yard. The Ministry in charge of Agricultural Production must pay an allowance to the owners of each field. The money infused must not be so small that it would be tantamount to exploitation; neither must it be so much so that we end up offering a product that is too expensive.

In the United States, it is impressive to see states that have very cold winter temperatures, like the state of Nebraska, having Agricultural Production. The farmers know that they have little time for cultivation — a little close to 3 months per year. They know exactly when to prepare the land, when to plant grains and when to harvest. They must complete everything before winter. Our country Haiti, on the other hand, enjoys a tropical temperature. We can work on our land throughout the year. We have enough rivers in Haiti to not have to depend on the whims of the rain to water the land.

We have seen from the "formula of development" that the reduction of imports is one of the means of arriving at a positive A. Even if we cannot compete with the United States in the agricultural domain, we can still produce enough to not have to import from other countries. Haiti has no reason to import rice, maize, fish, salt or sea food like fish from foreign countries. Someone who lives in Haiti must be able to go to a supermarket and buy food products at the local price.

Figure 19: Rice field at L'Acul du Sud after the application of the formula

Figure 20: The city of Cap-Haitien after the application of the formula

Haiti: A Sleeping Economic Giant

Haitians must not count on only agriculture to develop the country. Of course, we have a very strong point with which we can compete against any country in the Americas. By using it, Haiti can become one of the richest countries. China has used this power and its growth in the economic sphere is very interesting. We can do better than China. The strong point is what we call "the Haitian labor force".

Before we see how we have an advantage over a lot of rich countries today, including the United States, we are going to take into account two schools of thought adopted by people who are not qualified to hold leadership positions in Haiti. These schools of thought prove to us that these leaders do not have the slightest idea of the existence of the "formula for the development" of Haiti. After listing them, we will see together why these pseudo-solutions are disastrous to the country's economy:

- Waiting for economic aid from another country
- Allowing foreign companies to invest in Haiti.

Figure 21: City of Gressier after the application of the formula

The negative effect of depending on foreign aid

If the people vote for a head of state whose program is to go asking for aid from foreign countries, he and the people who elected him have no idea how the "formula for the development of Haiti" works. He and the people who elected him would sink Haiti deeper into the abyss of misery.

A country could give us aid. In fact, Haiti has always received aid from foreign countries. Haiti has been receiving food from foreign countries for a long time. Is it not a great generosity on the part of these donor countries? Yes, of course. Is there still hunger in Haiti? Yes, of course.

International organizations have also helped Haiti to increase its literacy rate since many years ago. Must we not be grateful to these people who came to help our children out of a good heart? Of course, we should. Are there still illiterate people in Haiti in 2015? Of course, yes.

According to a report published by the United Nations in 2011, the literacy rate in Haiti was 62.1%. On the other hand, in 1960, the literacy rate in Cuba was 60%, a level lower than Haiti's in 2011 (62.1%). In only one year, from 1 January 1961 to December 1961, the literacy rate in Cuba increased to 96%.

To accomplish something similar, Haiti must count only on Haitians. In fact, it is the responsibility of Haiti to feed the Haitian people. It is the responsibility of Haiti to give medical care to Haitian patients. In essence, the leader who can carry out the development plan for Haiti is the one who does not base his political program on the collection of international aid; the ideal leader for Haiti is far from being a professional beggar.

Figure 22: The road to Jacmel after the application of the formula

As a general rule, the aid which we receive from another country always causes more evil than good. It is very easy to confirm this golden rule given that Haiti has based its policy in favour of foreign aid. Let us take the example of the BCG vaccine which the United States had given to Haiti. A lot of Haitians have a "lump" somewhere on their arms which is a result of the BCG vaccine. In essence, we have become the subject of an American experiment: it is preferable to experiment on human beings than on animals. When the results were not satisfactory, they did not administer it to American children.

Furthermore, the first Haitian child to be injected had to have a contagious fatal illness to infect other children because they used the same syringe for all of them. Could we conclude that the Americans are evil because of this? The answer is no. If we don't respect ourselves, nobody would respect us.

By understanding the "formula for the development of Haiti", we can easily understand that the food-producing countries have techniques to increase their exports. One of the ways is to donate pills that will increase appetite to the inhabitants of the country to which it wants to sell its food products. The people who take them will have more appetite and will, therefore, eat a lot more food. To the extent that the number of people taking these pills increases, the exports of this producing country will increase to the same extent.

If a petroleum-producing country wants to increase its exports, it is capable of donating, for instance, diesel engine power plants. The importing country must, therefore, buy more petrol.

It is imperative that Haiti applies the "formula of development". By doing so, all Haitians will understand that the success of Haiti rests on a triangle whose three dimensions are:

- Haiti must **produce** a lot
- Haiti must **export** a lot
- Haiti must **import** little

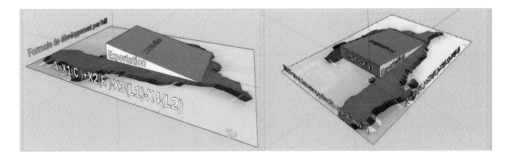

The negative effect of allowing foreigners to invest in Haiti

If the program of the Head of State is to encourage foreigners to invest in Haiti, it proves that he has a different idea of the plan for the development of Haiti.

The foreign person or corporation which comes to Haiti in order to invest money has only one goal: to make money. He is going to make money using the resources that Haiti has, i.e., the resources from which that investor would make money belong to Haiti. The political leader of Haiti, not knowing how to use these resources, has given it to someone else to exploit.

Do we remember Reynolds Metal Mines Inc.? They exploited bauxite at Miragoane from 1960 to 1980. A total of 13.3 million tons of bauxite were sent to Corpus Christi, Texas in the United States. Yes, they provided jobs to some Haitians during the exploitation at the mine. However, Miragoane has not had any benefits from this natural wealth, neither has Haiti. Miragoane is not even categorized as one of the cities that have the best infrastructure in Haiti (if there was any).

As with the example of bauxite at Miragoane, the Haitian labor force is our mine to transform our negative A into a positive A. By inviting foreign firms to invest in Haiti, they provide some jobs to some Haitians, but it is to the economic advantage of these firms, not Haiti's. They will earn what Haiti would have earned if it was a producing country.

Let us take the example of Venezuela which has underground petrol. From the moment the country took the initiative to remove foreign hands from the production of petrol, it took a positive turn. It should be underscored here that to exploit a mine, if we don't have Haitians who are qualified to occupy the key positions, we must employ foreigners while we train a group of Haitian professionals to occupy these posts. In the same way, in order to make our factory function, if we don't have enough competent Haitians for the key positions, we need to hire qualified foreigners to fill these vacant posts while we train a group of Haitian students.

Figure 23: Mome Tapion Tunnel after the application of the formula

The positive effect of using the Haiti's human mine

To see more clearly how Haiti is such a precious mine, let us compare 3 producing countries: the United States, China and Haiti. A very important point that should be underscored is that, to a large extent, the price of a finished product depends on the cost of labour. In other words, in an industry, the salaries of the employees largely determine the cost of the final product.

As strange as it may seem, the United States, Canada and many other advanced countries cannot compete with Haiti in the area of industrial production. Haiti is an enormous latent economic power. Haiti has this economic capacity, not because of its geographic position or its land area, but because of its inhabitants: the Haitian is very intelligent, whether he is poor or rich, literate or illiterate.

Figure 24: The General Hospital of Port-au-Prince after the application of the formula

The minimum wage per hour in the United States is $7.25. They might increase it to $10.10 sometime soon this 2015. In China, the region where labour is most costly is Beijing at US$2.73 per hour. In Haiti, we just increased the minimum wage to US $5.11 per day. The minimum wage per hour in Haiti is, therefore, about $0.65.

To better understand how Haiti is a "great sleeping giant", we establish a hypothetical factory in each of the following countries: the United States, China, and Haiti. We equip these three countries with the same technology. All three countries produce the same product: an electric oven. We will use the same number of employees in the three factories: 7000 persons.

Figure 25: Port-au-Prince's bicentenary after the application of the formula

In one month, the factory in the United States will spend $8,120,000.00 ($7.25 x 7000 employees x 160 hours = $8,120,000.00) to pay its employees.

In one month, the factory in China will spend $3,057,600.00 ($2.73 x 7000 employees x 160 hours = $3,057,600.00).

Every month, the factory in China spends $5, 062,400 ($8,120,000.00-$3,057,600.00) less than the one located in the United States.

In one month, the factory in Haiti will spend: $728,000.00 to pay its workers.

$0.65 x 7000 employees x 160 hours = $728,000.00

Every month, the factory in Haiti will spend $7,404,600.00 less than the one in the United States ($8,120,000.00-$728,000.00), which is nearly 11 times less than the total monthly expenditure in the United States.

Table 1: Monthly Expenditure on 7000 employees (3 identical factories, 3 different countries)

Pays	Par heure	Par Mois
Etats-Unis	$7.25	$8,120,000.00
Chine	$2.73	$3,057,600.00
Haiti	$0.65	$728,000.00

This implies that if an electric oven manufactured in the United States costs US $72 per unit, in China, it may cost $45 and in Haiti, it may cost up to $16 per unit.

The Haitian cost of labour is cheaper than that of China and a lot cheaper than that of the United States. Whenever the majority of Haitians understand the "formula for the development of Haiti", they would have the capacity to choose leaders who make decisions which favour their country. Besides, everybody who thinks he is incapable of applying the formula for the development of Haiti must not accept any leadership position in Haiti.

Unfortunately, we find that there are people who cannot apply the "formula for the development of Haiti" who still force themselves into leadership positions in the country. It is one of the reasons why, before the elections, the voters must assimilate this formula and discover those who cannot do anything for the country.

Figure 26: Jacmel apartment building after the application of the formula

Electrical Induction Explained

According to the formula, to transform a negative A to a positive A, it is compulsory to minimize importation to Haiti. Petrol usage would necessarily be the first product to be reduced.

The replacement of petroleum with electricity would greatly decrease imports of petroleum products into Haiti. We have to use electric ovens in our kitchens. By doing so, we would catch two birds with one stone: we would not need to cut down trees to cook our food directly or to make charcoal. That would also help us to control the problem of erosion in Haiti.

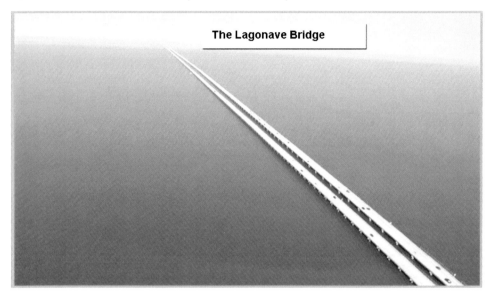

Figure 27: The bridge that leads to Lagonave after the application of the formula

Figure 28: The city of Grand-Groave after the application of the formula

To produce electricity, petroleum products may be used. However, we have no interest in importing petrol to produce our electricity. Rather, we will use alternative means to produce it. The use of electricity is so important in Haiti that we must explain it briefly.

To understand the production of electricity better, we must first understand electromagnetic induction. Electromagnetic induction was discovered in 1831 by an English scientist named Michael Faraday. We will try to illustrate magnetic induction in a simple way.

Let us assume that our hand is wet and that we have shaken it over somebody's face. What would happen to this person's face? There would be drops of water on his face. The wet hand represents a magnet, the person's face is the electric cable and the drops of water are what we call electric current. For water to be transferred to the face of the person, in other words, for electricity to pass through the electric cable, movement is necessary.

To increase the number of drops which fall on the face of the person, or according to our analogy, to produce more electric current, we can play around with 3 factors:

- A bigger wet hand.
  The wet hand of a child will hold less water than the wet hand of an adult man. In the case of electricity, a more powerful magnet would generate much more electricity than a less powerful one.
- A smaller face that would take fewer drops of water than a really big face.
  In the case of electricity, for the electric cable to take more electric current, more electric wire has to be wound. This is what is called a "coil". This coil can carry more electricity than an ordinary cable.
- The faster-moving hand that generates a greater magnitude of water.
  By analogy, the more rapidly rotates the magnet close to the coil, or the faster the coil is turned near the magnet, the more electric energy can be generated.

Figure 29: Croix-des-Bouquets factory after the application of the formula

Electricity Generation Explained

In the image below, we can observe magnets oriented in the direction of the south and north poles, between which there is a coil. At the moment of making the coil rotate by turning the handle, electric current is generated in the metal wire at the other end. This arrangement is called an "electric generator". A bulb attached to these wires would light up as long as we continue to turn the handle at the other end.

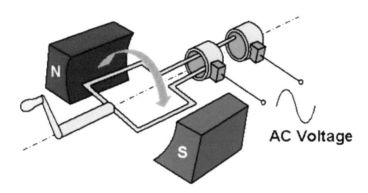

All systems for generating electricity use this electric generator model. There are obviously exceptions, some of which are:

- The solar system uses the principle of semiconductors provided in solar panels to produce electricity. This system has no moving parts.
- Batteries convert chemical energy into electrical energy.
- Nuclear cells also produce electricity by disintegration.

Figure 30: Leogane National School after the application of the formula

---

Physical force would be needed to turn the handle of the generator at one end in order to produce electric current at the other end. The handle of the generator may be turned by hand but before long, one would get tired. It should also be noted that to produce electricity in a city, we would need a high-capacity generator equipped with powerful magnets, with a high-capacity coil and a handle that is able to turn at high speeds. The human hand cannot do this work. Other forces must, therefore, be found.

The physical force that allows the generator coil to rotate can be a petrol engine. Many of us are used to what we call "delco" in Haiti. They use the same principle. The petrol engine causes the coil to rotate in relation to the magnet and the outcome is the production of electricity in the metal wire.

The steam engine is yet another method by which the electric generator can be rotated. An engine uses the pressure of steam to rotate a shaft. This axle is attached to the shaft of the generator and it is then possible to produce electricity. In many countries like the United States, coal is burned and the steam is directed towards the steam engine that is attached to a generator in order to produce electric current.

Instead of using petroleum which is very toxic to health, another way is to use vegetable oil or biodiesel, or using fuel based on animal fat which is burned to kick-start a steam engine which will subsequently rotate the generator in order to produce electricity.

Another way is to make a generator work with the help of nuclear reaction. The heat required to generate steam is produced by a physical process called fission. The heat emitted by the fission of uranium fuel makes the steam engine rotate and indirectly rotates the generator to produce electricity.

Figure 31: A factory ar Mirebalais after the application of the formula

---

If a 10-story building were filled with coal, nuclear fuel that is the size of a briefcase would give the same amount of heat which this enormous quantity of coal would produce in order to make the generator work. Consequently, many countries prefer to use the system that is based on the production of nuclear energy. The major problem with the nuclear system is that we must get rid of nuclear waste because it is highly toxic.

Another way is to use propellers to capture fluids. The most common ones are:

- Water – channelled into propellers which rotate a generator to produce electricity
- The tides – sea movement rotates the propellers and produces electricity
- Wind – when it blows, the propellers harness it and rotates, thus they rotate a generator which produces electricity

In summary, to rotate a generator, we can buy products like gas, diesel, nuclear fuel and vegetable oil. It is also possible to use what nature has given freely: the wind, the tides and the sea.

Figure 32: The city of Cayes after the application of the formula

Producing Electricity in Haiti

To be consistent with the development plan for Haiti, we must use a freely available resource to produce electricity. One of the best ways of producing electricity for our country is the hydroelectric system. Whichever system we have, we must maintain it. Otherwise, it would be a loss. It we would repeat the bad experience we had with the Péligre hydroelectric plant.

In this system, water from the river causes the generator coils to rotate constantly to produce electricity. There is no need to spend on gas or diesel! Many rivers in Haiti are good candidates for this hydroelectric system.

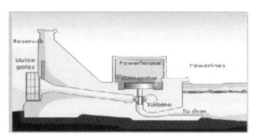

Figure 33: A schematic view of a hydropower plant

Another interesting way to produce electricity is to use tidal power. It makes use of the movement of sea tides to rotate the coils attached to a generator.

Another very efficient system, especially in coastal areas where the wind blows a lot, is wind turbines. The disadvantage is that the wind does not blow all the time. The best way to use it is to store the excess energy produced and to use this surplus when the wind is calm or not blowing at all. Batteries are the most common means of storage nowadays. These batteries are very costly, and the majority of them have a lifespan of 3 to 5 years. After the expiry date, we must still spend money to replace them.

Figure 34: Wind turbines at Grand'Anse after the application of the formula

An effective means of bypassing the use of batteries is to place wind turbines on a mountain at the base of which there is a river or the sea. The construction of a very big basin or reservoir on the mountain can be envisaged. Whenever the wind turbine produces excess electricity, it activates a water pump placed on the river or in the sea. The water pump will fill the big basin located on the mountain. Whenever there is no wind, the water from the reservoir will fall by gravity on propellers that rotate the generators and produce electricity without interruption.

Another way of producing electricity in Haiti would be the use of solar energy. Haiti is tropical; it enjoys abundant sunshine. This system does not use electric induction like with the case of the generator; it does not have moving parts, which is a big advantage. However, the inconvenience is that this system is not so efficient, and we would need big solar panels to supply electricity to the whole city. Taking into account our limited territory, it is preferable to use it in homes in order to reduce the demand for electricity in our country.

Pumped storage power plant du Cap Haitien

Housing

Since our territory is small, most buildings must be built vertically. An edifice can have between 60 to 100 storeys. It is compulsory that the construction of buildings complies with regulations for cyclones and earthquakes. When we talk of regulations for earthquakes, it is good to remember La Fontaine's fable *The Oak and the Reed*. The oak is strong and it can withstand powerful winds while the reed is flexible and, therefore, it bends at the slightest breeze. However, when they are both beaten by a powerful wind, the oak which cannot resist it breaks while the reed bends. After the powerful wind has passed, the reed returns to its initial position. In the same way, it is preferable that buildings are constructed in a strong, but particularly flexible fashion.

Figure 35: The city of Miragoane after the application of the formula

A building with a fixed foundation moves with the movement of an earthquake and may suffer enormous, irreparable damage, even if it is extremely strong. In order to minimise damages caused by earthquake to a structure, we can use several techniques. One technique is the use of an isolator. Isolators work in a similar way to a car's suspension. The suspension reduces the jolts that a passenger feels when the car moves over rocky, uneven roads.

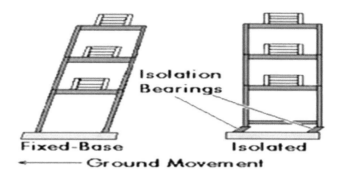

Isolation
Bearings

Fixed-Base   Isolated
Ground Movement

Isolation is a technique that was developed to minimise damage to buildings during an earthquake. The foundation isolation technique makes it possible for a stonework or reinforced concrete structure to withstand earthquakes. When the earth shakes, the building shakes, too, but at a slower frequency. The isolator dissipates most of the quake's impact. The whole of the building moves in two planes, by a foot or more. Isolators can decrease the impact of an earthquake by up to 80%. The installation of the isolation device prevents the transmission of the vibration of the earthquake to the building.

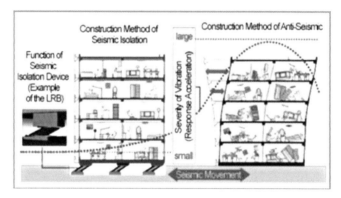

Some types of earthquake isolation systems use rotary roller bearings. The structure is made up of roller bearings, rails and slabs. This system works like a bearing to support the weight of a building and is also capable of displacing the building sideways without friction.

It should also be underscored that a skyscraper would be severely shaken during an earthquake or a storm by making it difficult to maintain the stability of the edifice and its occupants. The structure that controls the vibration has to reduce the vibration of the earthquake or strong wind by using the absorbent device on the building which not only prevents damages to the edifice, but also keeps people safe.

Figure 36: Residential apartments at Fort Liberté after the application of the formula

Within the framework of the formula, we have no interest in reconstructing Haiti with imported cement. To maintain a positive A, the cement must be made in Haiti. The owners of cement companies must be Haitians. The same applies to the steel. We must have our own Haitian steel mills.

Transportation

Haiti is a country that is blessed with a very dense population. Since the country will take the initiative to put in motion a development plan, we will begin to notice an increase in immigration. A lot of Haitians who currently live in foreign countries would begin to move back to the country. Haitians who currently contemplate living in a foreign country would change their minds; they would choose to live in Haiti.

To address this flow of Haitians who will travel around the country, a good public transportation system is essential.

Haitians are so brilliant that nothing can justify not manufacturing their own trains within the country. Even the Haitian who is deprived of all formal education exhibits an extraordinary level of intelligence. By applying the "formula for development", Haitians can use the same intelligence, but must focus in order to add more quality and lustre to their finished products.

The image below is a wheelbarrow that was made in Haiti. It is possible that the maker cannot read or write. However, almost all the mathematics and physics knowledge that is needed to construct an electric train have also been applied to this wheelbarrow. As an example, let us consider below how the maker has made use of the three laws of Newton in the construction of the wheelbarrow.

Jeremie, Grand'Anse
The city of poets

1. Literal expression of the first law

Every isolated body which is not subjected to any kind of interaction with other material object remains in its state of rest or rectilinear motion which it previously had.

$$\Sigma \vec{F} = \vec{0} \quad => \quad \vec{v} = \vec{Cte}$$

The maker of the wheelbarrow has two bars with which the wheelbarrow will be pulled. It can be predicted already that the wheelbarrow must obey Newton's first law. Without power supplied by a person, the wheelbarrow will remain at rest. The power of the person is essential to move the wheelbarrow.

2. The second law can be summed up in the following formula:

$$\sum \vec{F} = m \cdot \vec{a}$$

$\sum \vec{F} =$ Sum of the forces acting on an object in Newtons (N)

$m =$ Mass of the object in kilograms (kg)

$\vec{a} =$ The object's acceleration in m/s2

From the standpoint of inertia, the speed at a particular point varies in proportion to the sum of external forces applied to it and on the other hand, in proportion to its mass.

A person pulls the wheelbarrow. If the wheelbarrow is not loaded, an adolescent can carry it. If the wheelbarrow is loaded, a much more powerful person would have to pull it. The force with the driver exerts on the wheelbarrow would depend on its mass, on its acceleration by the load on it. To make it move faster, the driver must exert more force on the wheelbarrow.

Figure 37: The city of Arcahaie after the application of the formula

3. Newton's third law is also applied:

Whenever a body A exerts a force on a body B, the body B exerts a force of equal magnitude on the body A, but in the opposite direction.

$$\text{Force exerted by 1 on 2} \quad \text{Force exerted by 2 on 1}$$
$$\overrightarrow{F}_{1/2} = -\overrightarrow{F}_{2/1}$$

The wheelbarrow driver exerts a force of the same magnitude but in the opposite direction the force of the wheelbarrow. As a result, the heavier the load is, the more force the driver must apply to move it.

To allow the driver to pull the wheelbarrow, the person who made the wheelbarrow must use an equation from a branch of Physics that is known as "dynamics". This equation is called the "Equation of the coefficient of friction":

$$F_{Fr} = \mu \cdot F_N$$

F_{Fr} = frictional force in Newtons (N)
μ = co-efficient of friction (No unit)
F_N = Normal force in Newtons (N)

The force of friction depends on the coefficient of friction μ, which is determined by the two materials that are in contact, the texture and the smoothness of the surfaces, as well as the force which moves one towards the other, or the normal force, which is equal to the gravitational force "Fg".

The maker of the wheelbarrow has reduced the value of the wheelbarrow's coefficient of friction by putting wheels under it according to the equation above. He has, therefore, used the wheels on the wheelbarrow in order to reduce the coefficient of friction between the ground and the wheelbarrow. Without wheels, the driver would not be able to move the wheelbarrow with this entire load.

The construction of electric trains is an ancient technology that is easy to understand. In essence, the person who constructs carts in Haiti and the person who builds trains use almost the same technology. We can even build them in Haiti. With adequate training, Haitians can do wonders in the building of trains. The building of an electric train can be summed up in 5 steps:

1. Build a compartment where passengers stay: the coach.

2. We will add wheels to this compartment.

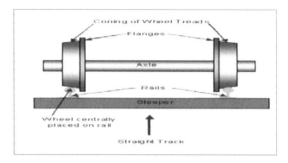

3. We will put one or several electric motors to these wheels.

4. A means of powering the electric motors.

5. Rails on which the wheels would rest on the railway track.

Waste Management

By the time the "formula for development" starts being applied, almost everything in Haiti would increase: people, vehicles, roads, work, money, food, potable water, schools. Unfortunately, the trash in the environment would increase, too.

To get rid of waste, waste disposal sites should be put in place. The landfill method is very common in most countries, including the United States. This method involves burying the waste in a big field. The dumped waste is usually compacted to increase its density. Great care must be taken because waste will naturally attract animal pests such as mice and rats.

The landfill method is not suitable for Haiti considering our limited territory. We need land for our houses, our schools, our office buildings, our factories, our roads, our hospitals, our churches, our recreation parks, our food plantations, our trees, but not for the disposal of garbage.

A better method of waste disposal in Haiti is incineration, more precisely, incineration with the recovery of energy. In general, incineration facilities do not need as much land as landfill sites. Incineration with the recovery of energy is in fact a "waste-to-energy" technology.

Incineration is the thermal destruction of waste. Modern incineration systems use high temperatures, controlled airflow and an excellent mixture to change the chemical, physical or biological character or the composition of residual materials. New systems are equipped with antipollution devices to capture particles, gaseous emissions and contaminants.

Incineration can be adapted to the destruction of a great variety of waste. This includes domestic waste, industrial waste, medical waste, sewage, Superfund sites and liquids as well as hazardous waste (liquids, coal tar, sludge, solids and chimneys) generated by industries. Contrary to other methods of waste disposal, incineration is a permanent solution. The principal advantage of incineration is that the process really destroys most of the waste rather than getting rid of them and preserving them in the process.

Incineration takes place inside an "incinerator", which can be understood more precisely as a furnace where waste is burned. Incineration transforms waste to gas and inert mineral ash.

The gas produced from incineration can be used for the production of electricity. Incineration generally involves the burning of waste to boil water. The steam from the water will power generators which will produce electric energy, which will be used in homes, businesses, institutions and industries.

The heavy ash is that which remains after the waste has been burnt in an incinerator. It is an inert and compactable granular material, which can be successfully used as a total replacement in the making of roads, particularly as the foundation of the road.

What is the best way for Haiti to collect waste? There are conventional methods for the collection of waste by which waste disposal trucks would go round residential and public areas to collect waste. However, the most convenient method for Haiti is the "collection of waste by automatic vacuum aspiration" which uses air suction in a closed network of underground pipes to transport waste into a central area from points of collection scattered all over the city.

There are various advantages of collecting waste by a vacuum suction:

- The elimination of undesirable odours which are generally associated with disposal in containers;
- Reduction of emissions from vehicles that gather waste;
- There are no traffic hold-ups in the system, even during rush hour.

A Proposal for How to Put in Place the Formula for Development

To understand and apply the "formula for the development of Haiti" is not only the business of the President, but it concerns all Haitians that live in the country and abroad. The first step would be to choose a group of about 15 people whose decisions would not be influenced by any government. This group of individuals could be called "the organizers" and would be made up of doctors, engineers, agriculturists, teachers, managers, accountants, technicians and others. They will prepare a list of products that will be profitable for production in Haiti.

These organizers will make their decision based on the "formula of development" for Haiti.

- The initial capital that is needed to begin to work
- The quantity of products that we can provide per month
- The choice of markets to which we will supply these products
- The number of employees that would be needed in the production chain
- The profitability of production

Figure 38: The city of Lascahobas after the application of the formula

For a long time, Haiti has always based its development program on aid from foreign countries. For this and other reasons, no country would want to lend us money. It is the responsibility of Haitians to invest in their country.

Let us assume that the initial cost of constructing and operating a workshop is $20,000,000.00. One way of getting this money is to find 5,000 Haitians who could invest US $4,000. We could also find 2,000 Haitians who could invest $10,000.00. The investors must be aware that the money invested will increase or decrease depending on the way the manufactured product is sold on the local and international markets.

Let us consider the case of a workshop which makes LED lamps. Haitians themselves must be the first customers. We must learn to appreciate our own products and encourage foreigners to use them. We buy our products, not only because they are Haitian products, but also because our workshops make good-quality products. The quality of our products must be the priority of our factories: this is a good way to remain competitive.

The Haitian investors will deposit their money in the Central Bank of Haiti. Ideally, it should be a central bank that does not belong to the "Rothschild family" but a central bank which is the exclusive property of the Haitian government.

The organizers are the ones who will choose the type of product to be manufactured in Haiti. If the product is not sold as it should be, investors risk losing all the money they have deposited. To encourage organizers to make a responsible choice of product, they will be affected positively or negatively if the product succeeds or fails in the market. To this effect, the organizers will receive a basic salary which is 20% of their total salary. The remaining 80% will depend on the monthly success or failure of the selected products.

Another group of persons must be chosen to make up the human resources department. This group will choose people who will head each workshop. To encourage the human resources department to choose the most capable leaders and not on the basis of friendship, family ties or sentiments, they will receive a basic salary that is 20% of their total salary. The remaining 80% would depend on whether the administrative achievements of the selected personnel turn out to be good or poor.

A third group is the inspectors, which is separate from the organizers and the members of the human resources department. The operations of the workshops will be inspected, as well as the quality of the manufactured products. They monitor the production of the workshop. They check the records of expenditures in each workshop. The inspectors also receive a basic salary that is 20% of their total salary. The remaining 80% will depend on the monthly success or failure of each workshop assigned to them.

Every employer must offer his full-time employees a health insurance and a retirement plan. If the full-time employee elects to purchase shares in a Haitian company, he will choose the amount of money he wants to be deducted from his monthly salary and the employer will give him an amount that is equal to his deduction. Thus, if the employee wants to deduct $30 from his monthly salary, the employer would also give $30. Therefore, the employee would invest $60 monthly, which is made up of the $30 deducted from his salary and the $30 which his employer gives him.

By applying the formula, we can truly sing this poem by the Haitian musician, violinist, poet and composer Dr. Louis Achille Othello Bayard:

Ayiti cheri pi bon peyi pase ou nanpwen
Fòk mwen te kite w pou mwen te kap konprann valè w
Fòk mwen te manke w pou m te kap a presye w
Pou m santi vreman tout sa ou te ye pou mwen
Gen bon solèy bon rivyè e bon brevaj
Anba pyebwa ou toujou jwenn bon lonbraj
Gen bon ti van ki bannou bon ti frechè
Ayiti Toma se yon peyi ki mèchè
Lè w lan peyi blan ou gen yon vye frèt ki pa janm bon
E tout lajounen ou oblije ap boule chabon
Ou pakab wèklè otan syèl-la andèy
E pandan si mwa tout pye bwa pagen yen fèy
Lan peyi mwen gen solèy pou bay chalè
Diran lane tout pye bwa ap bay lonbraj
Bon briz de mè toujou soufle sou no plaj

Ayiti Toma se yon peyi ki mèchè

Kon w lan peyi blan ou wè tout figi yon sèl koulè
Lan pwen milatrès bèl marabou, bèl grifonn kreyòl
Ki renmen bèl wòb bon poud e bon odè
Ni bèl jenn nègès ki konn di bon ti pawòl
Lan peyi mwen lè tout bèl moun si la yo
Sòti lan mès ou sòti lan sinema
Se pou gade se pou rete dyòl lolo
A la bon peyi se ti Dayiti Toma!
Lè w lan peyi blan ou pa wè mango ni kòk di tou
Lanpwen sapoti ni bèl kayimit vèt ou vyolèt
Lanpwen zanana ni bèl ti pòm kajou
Ki ban nou bon nwa pou nou fè bon ti tablèt
Ou jwenn zoranj ki soti an Itali
Men qui fennen qui toujou mwatye pouri
An Ayiti sa si bon se koupe dwèt
E sou se rapò nou bay tout peyi payèt
Lè w lan peyi mwen kote ou pase tout lon chemen

Se bonjou kompè e makomè e pitit la yo?Sa'n pa wè
konsa manyen rentre ti bren
Pou'n bwa ti kichoy pou nouj we de ti kout zo.
Fin bay lan men se rentre lan gran pale
Se politik se movèz sitiyasyon
Sa pou noufè se pou noupran li kou l ye
Men bon Dye si bon la ban nou benediksyon
Lè w ou lanpeyi blan ou pè promennen nwit tankou
jou Tout moun pè mache prese prese wa di se chen
fou Kote yo prale pou ki yap kouri konsa?
Yo pè pèdi tan yo pa janm di: kouman sa?
Lan peyi mwen moun pa rete avek lè
Genyen libète ou gen tan pou pran frechè
Kote ou pase se bonjou se bay lan men
Moun pa janm prese yo koze tout lon chemen
Lè w an Ayiti ou pa janm manke tan pou
soufle Sak pafèt jodi ou kap fè li demen si ou
vle Kan demen rive kel bon ou kel pa bon
Sa pafè anyen tout moun konn di bon dye
bon. An Ayiti moun pajanm dezespere
Nougen la fwa lan yon Dye ki pa janm manti
Nap fè jodi kan demen pa asire
A la bon peyi o mon Dye, se Ayiti!

About the Author

Ernst Etienne is Haitian by birth, even though he currently lives in the United States. Being a pastor's son, his childhood was expectedly marked with frequent relocations from one region to the other. Thanks to contact with people from different backgrounds, different cultures and different social statuses, these frequent moves have enriched his experience and opened up his mind. Thanks to his encounters with the poorest people, the richest people, people of the middle class, illiterates and learned people, he is perfectly knowledgeable about the needs and hopes of everyone in Haiti for building a prosperous country that is reoriented towards the future.

Ernst had his primary and secondary education in different towns in Haiti before leaving for a more international experience in Honduras and then in the United States, where he obtained a Masters degree in industrial engineering. Ernst is also an FAA-certified professional pilot and an FAA-certified flight dispatcher.

All of his experiences have contributed to the development of his curiosity and helped him to establish social ties with many people and most especially, to keenly know Haiti and all of its peculiarities very well.

Ernst is also a successful inventor of "Desfranches Range Extender Car", the "Desfranches Wind Turbines with vertical shafts" and the flying saucer "Anba-lakay".

CPSIA information can be obtained at www.ICGtesting.com
Printed in the USA
LVIW01n1141180917
549112LV00001B/8

* 9 7 8 1 5 1 9 2 8 7 1 0 6 *